EDITH CAVELL
Nurse, Spy, Heroine

Edith Cavell grew up in an age when the profession of nursing was regarded with contempt by nearly everyone. Born in England, she gave up a comfortable life as a private teacher in Belgium in order to become a nurse in the slums of London. Fate led her back to Belgium where, in the terror and bloodshed of World War I, she became one of the great heroines of the Western world. Sympathetically and dramatically, author Adele DeLeeuw reveals how Edith Cavell became an inspiration to every nurse who would live after her.

Illustrated by CHARLES BREY

Spies
of the
World

EDITH CAVELL

Nurse, Spy, Heroine

By ADELE DE LEEUW
Illustrated by Charles Brey

 G. P. PUTNAM'S SONS   NEW YORK

© 1968 by Adele DeLeeuw
All rights reserved
Published simultaneously in the Dominion
of Canada by Longmans Canada limited, Toronto
Library of Congress Catalog Card Number: 67-24147
PRINTED IN THE UNITED STATES OF AMERICA
10212

CHAPTER

I

THE NEW STONE vicarage in the sleepy village of Swardeston, England, was completed shortly before Edith Louisa Cavell was born there on December 4, 1865. She was named Louisa for her mother, a warm, friendly woman, younger than her husband, the vicar. The Reverend Frederick Cavell was tall and dour; a driving sense of duty, a harsh tongue, and a burning desire to save the souls of his parishioners made him a difficult man to live with.

The Reverend Cavell was proud of his new vicarage. He had laid out the plans for it himself and helped the local masons raise the walls. Its rear garden adjoined the cemetery where he often walked, talking aloud to the dead and planning his next sermon.

Edith learned to know her stern, forbidding father and her gentle, laughing mother, and love them both.

Her older sister, Florence, helped take care of her. Later, when Edith had a younger sister, Lillian, and a brother, Jack, she helped take care of them, reading to them and telling them stories. At an early age she showed an aptitude for drawing and liked to make sketches of birds, flowers and animals for the amusement of her sisters and brother.

In the summers she helped her mother gather berries in the garden and make pots of jam. Some were for their own table, but many were taken to sick persons in the village. Edith enjoyed carrying a pot of strawberry jam or a bowl of soup or a custard to someone who was ill and returning with the patient's thanks to her mother.

On Sundays, when there was a roast for dinner, her father often would carve off the best slices and lay them aside. "Take these, Edith, to Mrs. Jones," he would order. Before she could settle down to her own dinner Edith would have to carry the plate of meat halfway across the village. When she came back, her dinner would be cold. It seemed to happen nearly every Sunday, and she was always the one chosen to do it.

Edith loved the summers. It was good to be out of doors after the long cold days when the winds blew chill from the coast of East Anglia across the flat moors. In winter the house never was warm enough, for the Reverend Cavell believed in sharing his meager supply of coal with others not so fortunate. But in summer the family often went to spend a few weeks with Edith's aunt at the shore. Her aunt and uncle were fun-loving;

there was laughter in the big house all day long while the Reverend Cavell went walking. Edith's favorite cousin, Eddie, and she often took long walks together and had picnics on the cliffs. Slight and not very well, Eddie was sympathetic and quick to understand Edith. When she came back from an afternoon walk with Eddie her gray eyes had a fresh sparkle.

The Reverend Cavell was always worried about something. As Edith approached her twelfth birthday, her father was worried about a new Sunday School building. Where was the money to come from? Swardeston was a poor village where the men were laborers and farmers. Her father felt that he could not ask the people to give more than they were giving, yet he fretted about it endlessly.

Edith decided that something should be done. She wrote to the Bishop of Norwich—Norwich was a large town only four miles away where the cathedral was located—and told him of her father's plight. Would the Bishop please see to it that they had money to build a Sunday School?

The Bishop might have ignored her letter as the brash work of a young girl. But he was a kindly man, and he understood why she had asked. He wrote her in reply that he couldn't send all the money to the Reverend Cavell, but it was a worthy idea; if Swardeston could raise a portion of the money needed, he would see that they had the rest.

With the Bishop's letter in hand, Edith told her parents what she had done. Her father was astonished and angry. What would the Bishop think? But her mother thought Edith had a very good idea. "How do you plan to raise the money?" she asked.

Edith said, "I'm going to paint some little pictures and some cards. If people would buy them—even for a few pence—it would make a nice sum. At least I can try."

For weeks she drew and painted. Her mother helped her write notes to people asking if they would contribute something in return for a drawing. Her brother Jack carried the notes to the post office. The money began to come in—a shilling here, threepence there. The fund grew little by little until the Reverend Cavell was amazed and decided Edith had not been so foolish after all. When the sum was sizable enough, Edith wrote again to the Bishop reminding him of his promise. True to his word, he supplied the rest of the money needed, and by fall the new Sunday School was built.

Edith's schooling had been entirely at home, where her parents tutored her. Her father, teaching her in the quiet study, was secretly proud of her keen mind and willingness to learn. Money was scarce, but Edith's mother and father decided they must stretch every means to give her a better education. She must go away to a school. They had done all they could for her at home.

When Edith was eighteen she left the drowsy quiet of Swardeston for Miss Gibson's School in Peterborough. Laurel Court, as the school was called, was simply two old houses side by side; there were only twenty-five resident girl pupils, and presiding over the classes was a stout woman named Miss Gibson. Almost at once Miss Gibson was impressed with the quality of Edith's mind. Here was someone who wanted to learn, who was quick and intelligent. Edith liked the new life—her friendship with girls her own age, the challenge of books, learning French, at which she excelled.

The bells of Peterborough Cathedral sounded the hours, and there were matins and vespers and prayers, as there had been at home. But it was a wider life than Swardeston and the vicarage ever had offered. Edith always was grateful for the two years she spent there.

But now what could she do?

"I want to be useful," she told her cousin Eddie.

"What do you want do?" he asked.

"I don't know. Something where I can be of service to people . . . I wish I knew what it was."

"You'll find it, in time," he said.

It was Miss Gibson who arranged for Edith's first position. She had placed many of her girls in the kind of jobs that were offered to genteel young ladies in the 1880s. There was a wealthy family who needed a governess for their children. Would Edith take it?

It wasn't what she truly wanted. But what *did* she want? And she knew that she must earn her own living from now on. She knew, too, that she loved children and like being with them. She would do her best.

It was a pleasant household in which Edith found

herself. The children were devoted to her, as she to them, and the parents wrote Miss Gibson that they were delighted with her choice. Six uneventful years went by. As the children grew older, Edith wondered how much longer she would stay—and what she could do next.

Then a letter came from Miss Gibson. Edith read it excitedly. Friends of Miss Gibson's named Monsieur and Madame François in Brussels, Belgium, needed an English governess for their four children. Edith spoke French fluently and she had experience with children. Wouldn't this be an ideal position?

Here was a chance to see another world, a cosmopolitan world, so different from the quiet backwaters where she had lived. The prospect was thrilling. She wrote Miss Gibson that she would be able to get away within a month or so. It would be hard to leave the children, but a new life beckoned.

CHAPTER
II

IN THE François household in Brussels, Edith was like one of the family. It was a warm, closely knit family. There was much laughter during the long, hearty meals of rich food.

All the members of the family were surprised by Edith's seriousness, her frugal ways and quiet manner—above all by her total honesty.

One day not long after Edith arrived in Brussels, Madame François asked her to go to the door and tell a caller that she was not at home.

"Will you be home to dinner, Madame?" asked Edith.

Madame François smiled. "I'll be here all the time. I'm just going to write letters, but I don't want to see anyone."

Edith drew herself up stiffly. "I'll answer the door, Madame, but I cannot lie for you."

Madame François stared at her in surprise for a moment, then laughed. "You English!" she exclaimed. But there was admiration in her tone, and she never again asked Edith to tell a "white lie" for her.

Five happy years passed. The children were easy to manage and quick to learn English. There were pleasant walks, concerts, social gatherings. Sometimes life seemed almost too pleasant to the serious-minded Edith. She felt her life should have a greater purpose.

Then, one day, Edith received a letter from her mother that bore bad news.

Her father, whose heart was not strong, was ill with double pneumonia. Though her mother did not ask her to come home, Edith knew that she and her sisters and brother would have to take care of their mother. The Reverend Cavell had given away nearly all of his money; he even had deeded the vicarage to the church.

Edith told the François family the bad news, then packed her luggage. The family sent her off with their love, certain she would come back. But Edith felt it was the end of a chapter in her life. What would come next she did not know.

Her brother Jack met her at the station and her mother and sisters were waiting in the vicarage parlor. Their strained faces told her how much she was needed. Florence and Lillian were both studying to be nurses, but they were glad to turn over most of the decisions to Edith.

She did not take time to unpack. Jack was set to

heating sand in bags in the oven. Florence was sent out to buy a chicken from which to make broth. The Reverend Cavell was haggard and unconscious; the sound of his labored breathing filled the bedroom and he could not keep food down.

Edith piled the heated bags of sand around him and fed him broth from the tip of a feather, a drop at a time. While she caught a few hours of rest, her sisters took turns feeding him and changing the bags of sand.

In the morning he was better. He could keep down the broth and his breathing was easier. Day by day he regained strength until one morning he called Edith to him.

"I'm grateful to you for coming, daughter," he said feebly. It was the first time Edith had heard words like that from her father.

Suddenly she was heartened by the thought she was needed. She had found the work she wanted to do. In those days of endless vigil and care she formed a decision that changed her life.

She would be a nurse.

CHAPTER
III

E DITH WAS thirty years old when she made her decision. Wisely, she said nothing to her father. But when her mother heard about it she tried to dissuade Edith. It was one thing to nurse a patient for three weeks, but to enter a three-year training period at her age was something else again. And where would she get the money to support herself for that time?

Edith told her mother she had been well paid in Belgium and had saved a fair sum of money. She would not be dissuaded from becoming a nurse.

The profession of nursing was still in its infancy. Florence Nightingale, the aristocratic young Englishwoman who had nursed soldiers in the Crimea and returned to set up nurses' training schools in England, was an inspiration and a light. But there were few institutions as yet where a would-be nurse could get

real training. A trained nurse was suspect by patients and doctors alike. It was a long, arduous apprenticeship. In England the profession was hardly considered "respectable," and on the Continent a girl who entered nurses' training virtually gave up her right to be considered a marriageable person.

Edith presented herself to the London Fever Hospital, called The London for short. It was in one of the poorest sections of the city, near the docks. The streets surrounding it were drab, dirty, frequented by sickly children, sailor derelicts, and old beggar women.

Inside the ancient, grim building the walls were of whitewashed plaster, but the corridors smelled of carbolic acid and cabbage cooking. It was indeed a dreary place.

The head of the hospital was a dynamic young woman, twenty-six years old, named Miss Lückes, who had an enviable record of getting things done. She had accomplished wonders in the brief time she had been a directress. She worked for the dignity of the profession, insisting that nurses be accorded the respect due them as ministers to the sick. Gazing at Edith, she approved of her. Edith's eyes were straightforward and clear, her complexion good, her carriage upright. There was dignity in the little, five-foot-three woman who wore an unbecoming hat. She accepted Edith as a "pink."

"Pink" was the term for probationers, who wore pink uniforms. Graduate nurses wore green cloaks and bonnets.

Edith was taken to a dormitory room which she would share with three other probationers. It was a dingy room, though its walls were white, and had practically no heat. Edith was shown the wardrobe where she might choose a second-hand uniform or buy a new one. She chose a new one. Her day began early and ended late. When she wasn't studying she was supposed to scrub floors, polish brasswork, and tend the sick under the watchful scrutiny of more advanced nurses, who were usually hard taskmasters.

It was not an easy life. She ministered to the old, the sick, the criminal, the poor. She saw death so often in those first few years that she could hardly remember the first time she had encountered it. When she went on out-duty, she was appalled at conditions in factories and shops and squalid homes. Visiting the sick, she came to know London and to love it—its misty mornings, gray twilights, the long nights when she was on duty and only the bells of the city kept her company.

In 1897, when she had had two years of training, an epidemic of typhoid fever broke out in Maidstone, Kent. The hospital there could not handle all the cases and sent a call to London for volunteer nurses. Edith answered the call along with a few others. There were so many typhoid cases that emergency tents had been set up, and other patients were treated in their homes. Soon Edith began organizing the nurses into a more disciplined group so that they could care for as many patients as possible. She carried clothing and food to private homes, bathed fever-ridden patients, and held their hands in death. When the crisis was over in Maidstone, she had acquired new stature and understanding as a nurse.

Her first job after graduation from The London was as night supervisor at North St. Pancras Infirmary. There were two kinds of hospitals in England at the time: the voluntary hospitals, supported by private citizens, were free to turn away anyone too diseased or full of vermin; the Poor Law hospitals, supported by local Boards of Guardians, took in any patients who came to their doors. St. Pancras was a Poor Law hospital. It stood on a hill and was surrounded by gardens where the nurses often walked in their off-duty time. Edith's room was high up under the eaves. From its window she could look out across the roof-tops of London, listen to the evening songs of birds, and try to imagine she was in the country again.

Her work at The London had prepared her for the people who came to St. Pancras. Here there were even more patients. She hated to see a man still weak with fever go back to his dank little hovel and return to a job that had made him ill in the first place. It hurt her to send a small coughing child back to his dark, dirty slum home, where she knew there was not enough sunlight or food. She took clothing and bread and such delicacies as she could obtain into sooty little homes and wished she could do something about the crowded quarters, the overworked mothers, the anemic children. At first they could not under-stand why she came, but after a time they began to look on her with gratitude. She knew how to make friends in her calm, quiet manner as she showed mothers how to keep children cleaner or warmer, and how to cook simple, nourishing food.

She kept in touch with her friend and mentor, Miss Lückes, and in 1903 wrote her:

"You will, I think, be pleased to hear that I was elected yesterday to the post of Assistant Matron at Shoreditch Infirmary. I am glad to have obtained some day duty after my three years of night duty— also I hope the position will prove a help for the future, and the salary is larger than the one I am receiving at present. . . . I am glad to know I shall have supervision of the wards under Miss Inglis, and be able to teach the probationers to improve their work. I shall also have charge of the linen room and have to overlook the laundry. It will be a new experience, and I hope to learn much from it."

Miss Inglis proved to be a good supervisor, a merry woman with a ready laugh. She thoroughly appreciated Edith's meticulous work, her willingness and competence. But she never could feel close to her. Many people knew Edith Cavell, but no one ever seemed to know her well. Edith's reserve was like a wall; only her warm gray eyes revealed the heart hidden behind the wall.

In Shoreditch, Edith found herself doing much the same kind of work she had done at St. Pancras. She followed convalescent patients home—the children especially—in an effort to do something more for them and make their lot more bearable. It was discouraging, however, for so little really could be done. Nevertheless, she went to committees and influential persons, asking for contributions to send children away for a short time to the seashore or the country, where they could get fresh air and sunshine. When she could not raise enough money, she paid it out of her own pocket. She rejoiced to see the children return from their outings with a little color in their cheeks. And then she had to watch them sink back into the pathetic creatures they had been in the hospital—pale, sickly, undernourished. It was an endless uphill fight, with more defeats than victories.

Edith also instructed senior probationers, and found her drawing skill of help. Whereas she had drawn animals and landscapes when young, she now made precise anatomical drawings as she lectured in a clear, cool voice. It was work she thoroughly enjoyed. Perhaps, after all, her real lifework was to teach. When the offer came, she was ready for it.

CHAPTER
IV

THE OFFER came from an unexpected quarter. In Brussels there was a brilliant surgeon named Dr. Antoine DePage. He was small, thin, bearded, and had a quick temper which his attractive wife, Marie, could do little to curb. Dr. DePage, appalled at the state of medicine and nursing in Belgium, had an idea that consumed him. He would start a clinic and nurses' training school, too.

There were no nursing schools in Belgium. In fact, there were not many in all of Europe. Nursing was done chiefly by nuns who had little or no medical training. Nurses who had not taken religious vows were badly treated; sometimes their windows were stoned.

Dr. DePage was determined to improve the situation. He and his wife talked with prominent men and women in Brussels, urging them to sponsor a nurses' training school and support it. One of the members of a committee he had formed was Madame Graux, whose son Pierre had married Marguerite François. Marguerite never had forgotten the gentle Edith Cavell, her governess. When Marguerite told her mother-in-law about Edith, Madame Graux was so impressed that she urged Dr. DePage to write her.

It seemed to Edith Cavell that each of the turning points in her life had come as the result of a letter. Now the letter from Dr. DePage called for the biggest decision of all. She knew what lay ahead in Belgium. It would be difficult, uphill work. But it was a challenge and would demand all she could give to it. Here was a chance to put into effect her desire to teach, to build up the respect and dignity of the nursing profession, to administer a school and train young women as she knew they could be trained. She was forty-two years old. Behind her lay years of nursing experience. Now that experience could be put to good account in a different and exciting way.

She accepted Dr. DePage's offer and crossed the Channel again to Belgium. In a sense it was her "second country." She had come to know and love it while she lived with the François family. Now, seeing the parks again where she had walked with the children, sniffing the cleaner air of Brussels—how different from London!—she felt at home.

Dr. DePage was a man of boundless energy. He scarcely let Edith take off her coat and hat before he established her in the new clinic and told her of his plans. He had bought four brownstone houses, side by side, in a suburb of Brussels called Ixelles, and turned them into a clinic which would go down in history.

He called his clinic l'École Belge d'Infirmières Diplômées, but mostly people called it Dr. De Page's Clinic. Edith's room was small and bare, as her others had been. There was not enough heat, but she was used to that. At least her window looked out on a wide airy street. Birds sang in the trees, and bells chimed.

Edith and Madame DePage struck up a friendship almost at once. The doctor's wife knew how to handle her husband's rages and intemperate language, and she often interceded between Dr. DePage and his directress when their wills clashed. Dr. DePage was impatient of delay, of any kind of imperfection. In that respect, at least, they were in agreement. Edith Cavell had a passion for neatness, thoroughness, and self-discipline. In the first few months at the Clinic she was often near despair. There was not enough money; women members of the Committee had gone away for the summer; young women did not present themselves as probationers. The problems seemed endless.

Her old friend and mentor, Miss Lückes, back at The London, was of great help. Edith often wrote her for advice and begged her to send nurses or women wishing to train as nurses.

"The nurses [Edith wrote] sign on for five years— three for training and two to be passed in private or institution nursing, in the service of the school. At the end of that time they will receive their diplomas

24

and be able to leave. There are to be numerous lectures and in the second year the nurses will go to the Surgical Institute opposite for their surgical training."

Her wish was to draw Englishwomen to Belgium, to raise the standards of the nursing profession, and thereby help to weld the two countries together.

Delays and problems mounted. Only four Belgian girls responded as probationers. They giggled, resented the discipline, and arrived late on duty. Edith had designed for them a blue and white uniform with high white cuffs and a cap without strings. It was fresh and becoming, but when the girls went out on the street they were jeered at by workmen who called out, "This isn't carnival time!" It took courage for these girls to withstand the disfavor of friends, family, and Church. The Church looked with a jealous eye at the new training school; its officials pointed out that Edith Cavell was a foreigner and a non-Catholic in a Catholic country.

Edith found it hard to believe that there could be such a view of something she held so dear and so important. But she kept a tight rein on her emotions and tried not to antagonize committees, doctors or probationers. Often when she wanted to speak out she held her tongue. Tact was needed, she wrote Miss Lückes. She must above all things be tactful. If she could keep her four probationers until she had made them see the need for the qualities she insisted on, there would be hope of building her school and expanding the nursing service until it covered the country.

Often at night she lay awake planning how to meet

her problems and wondering if her dream would ever materialize. But when morning came, she was sure again. She talked with the girls, watched over their work, gave her lectures, consulted with the doctors, supervised the housekeeping, wrote letters to the parents of prospective probationers, wrote pleas to Miss Lückes for advice and nursing personnel, hurried down to her meals in the basement dining room, up again to her little office. In the evening she sometimes sat down at the piano and played hymns and familiar music for her girls. She would play for a while and then, without a word, leave the room and go to bed.

Her girls respected her and even loved her with a kind of awe. They did not quite understand her, but they recognized her sincerity. Long afterwards one of them said, "Next to other nurses, Miss Cavell made them seem so weak, so thin."

Gradually her nursing staff grew. More Belgian girls applied, several Dutch girls were taken on, some came from England, until the following year she could write:

"My new pupils are beginning to work. There will be seven to start the New Year, and I hope to have more before long. The four of the first year are now at the Surgical Institute, where I think and hope they will do well and begin to prove useful. . . ."

Her work kept her so busy there was little time for social life outside the Clinic. Though she did not make friends easily, she met in Brussels a Miss Carter, an Englishwomen working as a domestic science teacher, with whom she could visit and relax a bit. But with her subordinates and colleagues she remained aloof, impersonal—always kind and just, but, as they felt, remote.

Missing close human relationships, Edith found companionship in dogs. She had always loved them. Her parents had not allowed her to have one as a pet, but she had always made friends with dogs in the neighborhood and used them as models in her sketches. Now—as if they knew her weakness—half the stray dogs in Brussels, it seemed, found their way to the Clinic door. The staff had orders not to turn them away. They were fed and pampered; if mangy or ill, Edith brought them back to health.

One day a very special dog appeared and stayed— a medium-sized brown and white mongrel. She named him Jack, for her brother. Jack followed her everywhere and became her devoted friend and slave.

The Committee and some of the nurses were not happy about Edith's collection of dogs. They intimated that if she was such a stickler for hygiene, how could she tolerate these creatures in her establishment? But they knew better than to remonstrate too much. There was a look in Edith's eyes and a set to her lips that indicated how she felt. She would not turn away a stray. And Jack was her own particular dog.

Hospitals began to ask for nurses trained in her school. Then she was asked to find a matron for the Hospital of St. Jean, where most of the nurses were nuns. It was a compliment, and Edith wrote at once to Miss Lückes, asking her for the best possible person. Fortunately, Miss Lückes was able to send out a Miss Evans who, after working a while for Edith Cavell, went to her new post and spread further the English system of nursing.

By 1912 Edith directed not only the Clinic at 149 Rue de la Culture, but also a new hospital, St. Gilles, and a corps of nurses for private duty. She started a nursing magazine, *L'Infirmière*, and sent reports to the English magazine *Nursing Mirror*. In one of her articles she described the life of her nurses:

The nurses breakfast at 7 o'clock, wash their patients and give them their meals at eight. The house doctor comes at 8:30 and all the pupils accompany him on his round and carry out his orders when he leaves. The bathrooms are then tidied and the nurses dress, do their own rooms, and have lunch. At 12 o'clock dinner is served to the patients and at 12:30 to the nurses. As the early breakfast consists of coffee and bread and butter only, according to national custom, they are ready to do full justice to the soup, meat and dessert provided. At four o'clock they have tea, after the English fashion recently adopted here, the patients being served first. Beds are made, treatments carried out, and everything settled for the night when supper is served at 7 P.M. The nurses have their own supper at 7:30. It generally consists of meat, vegetables and cheese. Every nurse has two hours off duty, each day, a half-day a week, which is extended once a month to a whole day, and one month's holiday during the year.

There is a lecture given (in French) every weekday. The professors are well-known and their classes most interesting and suitable. The following subjects are taken the first year: anatomy and physics, hygiene, medical diseases, elementary pharmacology, care of the sick and sick nursing.

During the summer of 1912 Edith Cavell realized one of her ambitions. She had advertised for staff members in the *Nursing Mirror*, and then went to spend a holiday with her mother at a seaside resort in England. Her father had died in 1910, and she and her mother had drawn closer than ever. Edith always disliked to take time off from her duties, but she knew that unless she maintained her health she could not cope with her exacting work. It was while she was on vacation that she received an answer to her advertisement that struck her at once.

Elizabeth Wilkins wrote from her position on a hospital staff in Cardiff on the coast of Wales. She was throughly trained as a nurse and spoke French.

When Edith met Elizabeth Wilkins she felt confirmed in her first impression. Here was someone who would be her right hand. Like Edith, she had been strictly brought up, liked to work, and did not mind the restrictions and discipline of her profession. Edith arranged at once for Elizabeth to come to Brussels.

Elizabeth, who was called Sister Wilkins, fitted into the regime at the Clinic and nursing home with ease and was a devoted friend of Edith's all her life. It was as well they had found each other when they did, for now Edith was involved in another responsibility. Doctor DePage had decided to build a new clinic across the street from his first one. Edith visited the site every day, impatient to see it completed.

Meanwhile, her sister Lillian, who had married a Dr. Wainwright, asked her to take a yound friend, Grace Jemmett. During a serious illness Grace had been given morphine; when she recovered, she was an addict of the drug and needed to be watched over constantly. Dr. Wainwright felt that if Grace were away from her family and in the care of someone like Edith she might recover.

Edith knew that if she took in Grace she would be criticized even more severely than she had been for caring for stray dogs. But the idea appealed to her. Grace was young, lovely, in need of help. And she herself needed someone to love. The children in the hospital ward were always her special concern, but none ever stayed long. Grace, on the other hand, would be with her for a long time. When she met her, the comparison to a child was striking. Grace's air of innocence, her large eyes, her appealing ways touched Edith's heart; she decided to make her a member of the household.

On July 14, 1914, Edith went back to England for a visit with her mother. Mrs. Cavell was shocked to see how thin Edith was and how many gray hairs tinged the soft brown. During the vacation she seemed to grow younger and some of the sparkle returned to her eyes, which were as luminous and steadfast as ever.

Afterwards people who knew Edith wondered why she had decided to go home that particular summer. Unrest and fear were in the air. Two weeks previously a young Serbian had shot the Archduke Franz Ferdinand, who was heir apparent to the Austro-Hungarian throne, and his wife, a commoner. Surely Edith must have known what that action could lead to.

A shadow lay over all of Europe, a shadow that became a black cloud. Austria–Hungary declared war on Serbia on July 28. In August, Germany went to war with Russia and on August 4 moved against Russia's ally, France.

World War I had begun.

CHAPTER
V

EDITH COULD have stayed in England, as her mother begged her to do. As a trained nurse she would find plenty of work in her own country.

But Edith said that Belgium needed her more. She realized that if the Germans invaded France, England was bound by a treaty to aid France. And both England and France had agreed to defend the neutrality of Belgium.

When Edith landed in Belgium she learned that the Germans had already invaded the country. Cutting across neutral Belgium was Germany's easiest means of sweeping into France.

The Brussels railroad station was in chaos when Edith arrived. Troops were being transported, ammunition was being rushed to the front, while the Germans who were leaving the country huddled together over hastily assembled baggage.

Edith's German nurses at the Clinic were in tears. She helped them pack and took them to the station, then prepared the Clinic to receive wounded soldiers. Doctor DePage was organizing field hospitals near the front.

The next day England entered the war. But Edith, like many others, believed the war would be over in a few weeks.

At first everyone was confident. The English were coming to the rescue of France; together they would repulse the Germans and drive them out of Belgium. The days were sunny and warm, and hope ran high. Everywhere, people spoke with courage and optimism.

Then the important city of Liège fell to the Germans. The Belgians were stunned. Next Namur, another stronghold, was taken by the Germans. Stories reached Brussels of pillaging and burning, of women and children murdered, of villages destroyed. Nevertheless, people believed Britian would come to their aid and drive the Germans from Belgium.

Edith described in a dispatch to the *Nursing Mirror* how the Belgians met the supreme disaster—the fall of Brussels.

Brussels lay that evening, breathless with anxiety. News came that the Belgians, worn out and weary, were unable to hold back the oncoming host who might be with us that night. Still we held to the dwindling hope that the English army was between us and unseen peril. For several days all the entrances to the town had been held by the Civil Guard, who had dug trenches and lay in them night and day, but it did not need a soldier to see that they could oppose no possible resistance to the great army of the Kaiser. It was a grateful duty to take these brave men hot coffee and food to fortify them against the nights, already chilly, of late summer.

In the evening came the news that the enemy were at the gates. At midnight, bugles were blowing, summoning the Civil Guard to lay down their arms and leave the city. Many people were up through the dark hours, and all doors and windows were tightly shut. As we went to bed our only consolation was the certainty that in God's good time, right and justice would prevail.

On August 20th the sun shone out in mockery on our fallen homes; the last train left the capital at 6 A.M.; the rolling stock was shunted to Antwerp and the station closed. The King, the Royal Family, and the Government had left on the previous day and the wireless apparatus connecting this little land with its big possession in Africa had been blown up. Many people left the city by motor, and crowds thronged the square in front of the North Station, hoping for a chance to depart. All night long the wounded had been removed by ambulance to the station and sent away in safety to the last stronghold of Belgium. Later, we knew the city had been handed over to the enemy by its beloved [Mayor], M. Max—now a prisoner in Germany. In the afternoon, with much pomp and circumstance of war, the German troops marched into Brussels, and to the Town Hall, where the brave tricolor came down and the German stripes of black and white and red took its place. . . . The Belgian crowd watched this desecration in silence and with profound sadness; some wept, but for the most part they showed great self-control, and no word of abuse or hatred escaped them. The police moved about among them, exhorting them to calm and crying, "Patience, patience."

The troops are all in grey, with their brass helmets covered and their arms of dull steel. There are at least twenty thousand who entered the city that day and camped in it for the night. Some were so terribly stiff that they could scarcely walk, and many had their feet sore and blistered with their long marching in heavy boots.

On August 21st many more troops came through; from our road we could see the long procession, and when the halt was called at mid-day and carts came up with supplies, some were too weary to eat, and slept on the pavement of the street. We were divided between pity for the poor fellows, far from their country and their people, suffering the weariness and fatigue of an arduous campaign, and hate of a cruel and vindictive foe bringing ruin and desolation on hundreds of happy homes and to a prosperous and peaceful land. Some of the Belgians spoke to the invaders in German, and found they were very vague as to their whereabouts, and imagined they were already in Paris; they were surprised to be speaking to Belgians and could not understand what quarrel they had with them. I saw several of the men pick up little children and give them chocolates or seat them on their horses, and some had tears in their eyes at the recollection of the little ones at home.

From that day till now, we have been cut off from the world outside—newspapers were first censored, then suppressed, and are now printed under German auspices; all coming from abroad were for a time forbidden, and now none are allowed from England. The telephone service was taken over by the enemy, and we were shortly deprived of its use. The post, too, was stopped, and, though now resumed to certain towns and countries, all letters must be left open and contain no news of war, or of anything of importance. The few trains that run for passengers are in German hands, and wherever you go you must have, and pay for, a passport. No bicycles are allowed, and practically no motors, so that once busy and bustling streets are very quiet and silent. So are the people, who were so gay and communicative in the summer. No one speaks to his neighbor in the train, for he may be a spy. Besides, what news is there to tell, and who has the heart to gossip, and what fashions are there to speak of, and who ever goes to a concert or a theatre nowadays, and who would care to tell of their all-absorbing anxiety as to how to make both ends meet and spin out the last of the savings or to keep the little mouths at home filled, with the stranger so close by?

I am but a looker-on, after all, for it is not my country whose soil is desecrated and whose sacred places are laid waste. I can only feel the deep and tender pity of a friend within the gates, and observe with sympathy and admiration the high courage and self-control of a people enduring a long and terrible agony. They have grown thin and silent with the fearful strain. They walk about the city shoulder to shoulder with the foe and never see them, or make a sign; only they leave the cafés which they frequent, and turn their backs to them, and live a long way off, and apart. . . .

Edith and Sister Wilkins stayed in the Clinic while the city was taken over. But some of the nurses and the cook's children went up on the roof to watch the gray German hordes moving in mechanical precision down the boulevards. The sky was blood red, the crash of artillery incessant and terrifying.

Brussels became a gray city—gray with the uniforms of the invading army, gray with despair. Yet in the midst of sorrow and bewilderment, the spirit of the Belgian people rose to the surface.

To Edith's surprise and delight she recognized now the qualities she had learned to appreciate during years of living among the Belgians. They did not bow down to the enemy, but found ways of showing their independence.

It was forbidden to sing the national anthem. But

along the streets of Brussels people were singing it—one sentence at a time, from house to house. The German patrols were baffled and furious, but they found it impossible to punish any specific person. After all, no one person had sung the anthem—only a sentence of it!

On more than one occasion groups of citizens—as if by agreement—appeared wearing scraps of white paper in their buttonholes. The Germans had said contemptuously that the treaty with Belgium was "only a scrap of paper." By some mysterious conspiracy citizens would agree to set their alarm clocks for a certain hour. Troops patrolling the quiet, deserted streets would suddenly be assailed by a terrific clamor of bells. They would rush about, calling orders, hunting for the cause of the commotion—and, as suddenly, the bells would stop. Quiet would return, but at each window would be a grinning face. Other people found satisfaction in waiting for a patrol to pass, dropping a heavy saucepan tied to a string onto the pavement with a resounding bang. Before the patrol could turn, the saucepan was withdrawn.

Though they were small distractions, almost the pranks of children, they served to keep up spirits. Additional curfews were imposed, yet the incidents were repeated. If Germans entered a café, the Belgians left. In every way they could the people of Belgium tried to show their contempt for the enemy. The actual struggle to get the enemy out of the country was something else.

Edith Cavell and all English nurses in Belgium

were offered safe conduct to Holland. All refused to go. Some managed to get to France and joined the Red Cross there. But Edith felt her mission was in Brussels. She knew now how grim the situation was. Just before the fall of Brussels she had written her mother:

If you open this, it will be because that which we fear now has happened, and Brussels has fallen into the hands of the enemy. They are very near now and it is doubtful if the Allied armies can stop them. We are prepared for the worst.

I have given dear Gracie and the Sisters a chance to go home, but none of them will leave. I appreciate their courage, and I want you to let the Jemmetts know that I did my best to send Gracie home, but she refused firmly to leave me—she is very quiet and brave. . . .

If I can send my few jewels over, will you divide them between Flor and Lil, and please send Mrs. McDonnell my long gold chain, which she gave me, and a keepsake to Marion Hall?

I shall think of you to the last, and you may be sure we shall do our duty here and die as women of our race should die. . . ."

She gave the jewels in a little box to some friends she had met. When it became clear they could not get away, the box was returned to her. The letter itself never reached her family. It fell into the hands of a German officer, and not until he died twenty years later did it become public.

There were a few days of quiet and then, on August 25, the Germans doubled their guard on Brussels. No one knew why until that night when refugees, women and children, came pouring into the city from Louvain, a town to the east of Brussels. In Louvain the university had been destroyed, civilians shot. Edith was horrified at the firsthand accounts of German brutality. Families trying to escape had been forced back into burning homes. Women saw their husbands arrested as hostages. People were compelled to stand in line and watch mass executions in front of the station.

"Why?" she asked. "Why?"

Not until later did she hear the answer the Germans gave. German soldiers were looting some empty houses when they saw soldiers entering Louvain. Thinking they were Allied troops, the Germans fired on them. But it turned out they had fired on their own countrymen. By the time they discovered their mistake, half a dozen men were dead. Rather than admit their error, the officers in command said Belgian guerrillas had murdered some of the Kaiser's soldiers. They must avenge the attack—and the massacre at Louvain was the result.

It seemed, in the days that followed, that the Germans did not know where to stop. They felt they were on their way to complete victory. On September 20, German Red Cross nurses arrived in Brussels and took over the public hospitals. One atrocity after another was reported in the countryside. Edith did not have the heart now to join the other nurses in their evening talks. She was remote and withdrawn. Sister

Wilkins and Grace worried about her. There was plenty to do at Rue de la Culture, but how long could they last?

"I have seen suffering, poverty, and human wretchedness," Edith wrote, "in the slums of London but nothing I saw there hurts me the way it does to see these proud, gay, happy people humiliated and deprived of their men, their homes invaded by enemy soldiers that are quartered in them, their business ruined. I can only ask myself why, oh, why, should these innocent people be made to suffer like this?"

She wrote constantly at her desk in her cold little room. Indignation boiled in her and overflowed into conversation. She was always truthful; she must say what she believed. Her friends, the nurses, Sister Wilkins, all cautioned her to speak more prudently.

"In times like this," Edith Cavell answered, "when terror makes might seem right, there is a higher duty than prudence."

CHAPTER
VI

WHEN THE war broke out, Louise Thuliez, a young schoolteacher, was on vacation in the little village of St. Waast-le-Vallée. Suddenly the peace and calm were broken by men departing for the front, many of them never to return. Hordes of weary refugees swarmed past, driving their stumbling oxen, carrying a few household possessions, trying to quiet their crying children. She saw the retreating Allied army tramping through the dust. Worst of all, she saw the maimed and wounded Allied soldiers left to die.

Most of the village people fled with the other refugees. Cottage doors stood open, houses were deserted. Only a handful of people remained, but they were staunch of heart. They set up beds for the wounded, while the battered and weary soldiers, after a brief rest from days of grueling fighting, plodded on.

The next morning Red Cross ambulances came to pick up the wounded. But six British soldiers, too ill to be moved, were left. The ambulances would return, the drivers said. But they did not. Instead, German troops swarmed into the village. After a day of horror they moved on too, leaving a devastated village, fences trampled, livestock slaughtered, food stores sacked. All who remained were the few villagers—and the six wounded Englishmen.

Louise arranged to have the wounded men moved into the home of a friend, Henriette Moriamé. Together they took care of them. When Germans passed through occasionally, they did not bother with the wounded, who would only be a handicap if seized.

But Louise and Henriette knew the situation could not continue. As the men grew better, they were increasingly in danger. They must somehow be moved to safety. But how?

Near the village, in the beautiful forest of Mormal, was an ancient castle, the Château de Bellignies, where the de Croy family lived. The Princess Marie and her brother Prince Reginald had turned the château into a Red Cross hospital at the outbreak of the war. The Prince knew every inch of the countryside, so Louise went to him for advice. The Prince urged her to bring the men to the forest near the château if she could. No one knew better than he what danger this entailed. Moving through the forest, even at night, was risky. One might run into a German patrol at any time. Louise realized the danger too.

Two nights later, as soon as it was dark, Louise

and Henriette and the six men left the comparative safety of the Moriamé home and quietly disappeared into the forest, pausing at every sound. The two women promised to bring the men food and clothing and to care for them as best they could. They returned to the village about two in the morning and later in the day reported to the mayor that the six Englishmen had "escaped."

The men were safe for the time being, but soon the trees would be bare and their hiding place might be discovered. As it happened, Louise and Henriette realized, all too soon, that their men were not the only ones hiding in the forest. There were others, pitiful ones, who had been deserted by their armies in retreat. The fortunes of war had cast them aside, to fend for themselves as best they could.

Now Louise and Henriette's days were full. They made regular trips to the forest, always under cover of darkness, taking food with them. Gradually other villagers began to help them. Word of what was happening spread across the countryside. A band was formed to help the men living in dugouts and hollows covered with twigs. Plans were made, messages were carried, food was collected.

Louise learned to walk quietly and be wary of everyone and everything. She was the one chosen to get messages to the château, where a band of fugitives had already gathered, waiting for the strategic moment to escape.

She urged her own refugees living in the forest to be exceedingly cautious. They must avoid being seen at all cost. The men, living from hand to mouth, in constant discomfort and fear, promised readily enough. But sometimes they grew careless. The villagers nearby stared blankly at Germans who interrogated them—certainly not, of course not, there couldn't possibly be anyone in the forest! Even so, the Germans became suspicious. Louise was warned one Sunday morning at church that the Germans were sending reinforcements. The priest told her that men had been ordered to quarter the forest—to mark it off and search it inch by inch.

Louise knew there was no time to lose. By this time there were thirty men hidden in the forest whom she must help. She hurried into the forest to round up the hidden men and send them to the castle. In a heavy rain the men and Louise plodded to the safety of the château.

There the Englishmen held a council. They decided it was too much to ask young women to brave these constant dangers for their sakes. They would give themselves up, they told Louise the next morning. She was aghast. After having endured so much, how could they think of it? She was sure there was a chance of breaking through the lines on the farther side of the forest; they must at least try. She and Henriette would scout the land by day. If it was feasible, the men could make it by night. It meant walking twenty miles, but the women insisted they would do it.

The two young women set out at dawn and were back again by nightfall, almost too tired to walk. Yes, they had scouted the route. The men could certainly find their way to freedom, though it would be dangerous and difficult.

The captain in command of the group stepped forward. He could not permit his men to risk it, he said; they had decided to give themselves up. Louise Thuliez was near tears. If they would not make the dash for freedom, she said, wouldn't they at least consider going back into the forest and hiding as they had before? She and others would continue to bring them food and clothing.

The captain shook his head. He said he knew it was a futile journey. Besides, the weather—which had been kind until now—was turning. Louise looked out the window and saw snow falling. In the snow footprints could be read easily. The men no longer would be safe in the forest.

With tears she watched the men take their few belongings and march away to surrender to the Germans. They would be sent to prison camp—these gallant soldiers for whom she had hoped to win freedom. She vowed, standing at a window of the château, that from now on there would be no more surrenders. She would find other ways of helping men escape or return to their families.

It was the beginning of a plan which soon would involve Edith Cavell.

CHAPTER

VII

THE WINTER OF 1914 was bitter. Food grew scarce; coal was rationed; there were no lights except from kerosene lamps. But with the bitter weather, determination grew in the Belgian people. They would defy the Germans, and they would help others to defy them.

Life must go on. Babies had to be fed; the sick had to be cared for. The hospitals were filled with Germans as well as Belgians. Belgian women had begun to see that nursing was a profession of dignity demanding their best efforts. Even so, there were some who said they could not care for a German.

Edith Cavell allowed no such distinction among her nurses and probationers. She explained sternly that if a man was wounded or sick—be he German or Belgian or refugee or French—he deserved the best of care. Their mission was to tend the sick, to preserve life wherever they could. Did they understand? Even the most rebellious nurse found herself changing her viewpoint under that quiet scrutiny and authoritative voice.

But now Edith had a battle with herself. In the Clinic were a number of wounded Belgian soldiers. The Germans ordered that whenever a soldier left a hospital he must report to police headquarters. It meant, of course, that he probably would be sent to a prisoner-of-war camp in Germany—and possibly never be seen alive again. It was more than Edith could contemplate. She must have wrestled with the question for many a dark hour before she made her decision. Once made, however, she never deviated from it.

She called her nurses to her and told them, "When a man is ready to leave, you will give him directions to the nearest police station." They could hardly believe their ears. Would their directress turn over these poor innocents to the Germans? Then Edith went on, "You will also tell them that if they take another route they will come to the house of a friend."

The nurses did not dare ask who would give the soldier the name of the home of a friend. Who else but Edith Cavell herself?

"That way," said Edith quietly, "if the police ever question you, you will be able to say truthfully that you did direct the men to police headquarters. They can decide for themselves which way they go."

It was less than the whole truth, and she knew it. But it was the only thing to do. Had she not told her nurses—as she believed devoutly herself—that their mission was to save lives? There was more than one way of saving lives.

That was the beginning. Little by little, person by person, a network willing to shelter men trying to escape was built in Brussels. It was not an organized underground movement, as there would be in later wars. A baker might hide a man in his spare attic room; a boy on a bicycle might slip a note into a woman's shopping cart; a schoolboy might drop a word or two as he passed a stout gentleman out walking with his cane.

As the underground work spread, it linked up with the work being done by Louise Thuliez and Henriette Moriamé near the French border. Others were work ing there now, too. One was a mining engineer, Hermann Capiau. He and the Countess de Belleville— an old friend of the de Croys—served from the beginning as links in a chain that led to the Dutch border for many an Allied soldier.

The route Capiau had been using to cross the Dutch border was closed now. The only way of escape since the fall of Antwerp was through Brussels. It was a devious route and filled with danger, for it was longer and involved more people. But Capiau saw no other way to get his refugees out. He must establish contacts in Brussels for the safe conduct of his men.

There was no time to lose. A friend of his, a Monsieur Libiez, had been hiding an English officer and a sergeant in his home when word came that the Germans would make a house-to-house search in his district. In desperation Libiez went to Capiau, who in turn tried to contact people who might help. But he had no luck.

Capiau went to Brussels, where someone referred him to Madame DePage. As a doctor's wife she might be willing to help.

Madame DePage was afraid to risk taking in soldiers—not for herself, she said, but for the sake of her children. She thought a moment.

"The men are English?"

Capiau nodded.

"Then I think I know someone who might help."

She handed him a slip of paper on which she had written a name. It was Edith Cavell, 149 Rue de la Culture.

Capiau made his way through the dark, deserted streets to the address he had been given. He had to dodge German patrols; every time he heard footsteps he wondered if they were following him. But he had a mission, an urgent one.

The nurse who let him in was suspicious of him. She made him wait in the hall till she took a message to the directress. Edith Cavell had never heard the name Hermann Capiau. She, suspicious too, ushered him into a small room where they could talk privately. When he gave her the note from Madame DePage, Edith recognized the handwriting. She felt Madame DePage would not have sent anyone who was not trustworthy.

"What do you want me to do?" she asked Capiau.

He told her he had two wounded Englishmen hidden in a convent. He could not leave them there.

If she could return these men to health, they would not trouble her any longer than necessary. They were anxious to rejoin their comrades.

Edith stood motionless, debating her course. There was never any question really as to what she would do, but she went over in her mind what this step would mean. Then she told Capiau to bring the men to the Clinic under cover of darkness next day. She would have a place for them.

The men were smuggled in and hidden in the cellar. But next morning when one of the probationers went down early for tea and bread, she was terrified at sight of the men. While she stood transfixed against a wall, a cheerful English voice called out, "Hello, nursie!"

After that, of course, there was no keeping the presence of the men a secret. But all the nurses and probationers, excited and anxious as they were, understood the necessity for maintaining strict silence and acting as if they knew nothing. Life was grim enough for everyone. Now, for all of those at the Clinic, it had also become dangerous.

Several nights later Edith asked Sister Wilkins to bring some packages of food to her room. Sister Wilkins knew better than to ask questions, but she had her suspicions. When it was quiet in the house, she heard Edith go downstairs, and a little later the front door closed quietly. Sister Wilkins lay wide-awake until early in the morning when she heard the door close again, just as softly, and a light tread on the stairs. Edith Cavell had returned safely. Sister Wilkins could breathe again. The two Englishmen had been delivered—where? At least they were safe for the time being and on their way out of the country.

In the morning it seemed to Sister Wilkins that Edith looked thinner, older, and was even more quiet. She ate her early breakfast in silence in the dimly lit dining room and went upstairs without speaking to anyone.

Later in the morning Capiau was there again. Miss Cavell had been so kind as to shelter two of his men. Now he had eight more. Could she take them in? Edith nodded. She knew now that she was committed. How could she refuse to help these men since she had helped the others?

The Clinic grew crowded. When the beds were full, they were hidden in the attic or cellar. The Prince de Croy came to see her. He had heard of her wonderful care and assistance to escaping men. Would she do one more thing—take into her nursing home the men that he sent her? The password would be Yorc—his name spelled backward.

A circle was closing around her. When Louise Thuliez called later, in February, 1915, the circle was complete. She was part of the rescue work of the underground. Louise Thuliez arrived with eight men whom she left with Edith in broad daylight. No sooner had she come than she departed, like a shadow. There was still so much to be done! She and her friends were scouring the woods daily for deserted soldiers who had escaped the Germans and were afraid for their lives.

With the growing number of escapees in her nursing home it was harder and harder for Edith Cavell to make ends meet. It was difficult enough to get food under any circumstances; even water was rationed now, and the Germans were making life more difficult by the day. A new German governor-general was sent to Belgium, a man who seemed to glory in grinding down the Belgian people. One of his rules was that any British soldier who did not give himself up would be declared an outlaw and shot on sight. The Germans were well aware that soldiers were escaping, literally through their fingers, and they were angry about it. The Belgian resistance was growing, and General von Bissing was determined to crush it.

But it was not an easy task. The spirit of the Belgians seemed to grow stronger with every hardship put upon them. A tonic to their courage was the publication of a secret newspaper, *La Libre Belgique*, which appeared once a week. It appeared not only in the mailboxes of Belgians but on the desks of the German high command, including General von Bissing. The Germans, infuriated, scoured the country to find who was responsible for its publication and where it was printed. Try as they might, however, they could not find the resistance printer or the various people who distributed it. Finally, special police were sent from Berlin to try to crack the problem. The paper mocked the Germans in every possible way; once a week the Germans became enraged while the Belgians smiled happily and felt a renewal of their fighting spirit.

The dreary winter wore on, one hardhip following another. Edith Cavell spent increasing hours at her desk, working on her account books, wondering where she could find the money to keep open her nursing school and feed her "patients." More and more men were turning up—English, French and Belgian soldiers, along with German soldiers who must also be nursed back to health. Some needed clothing before they could be sent on their way out of the country; she must find money somehow for that. Food grew scarcer and more expensive, yet they must be well fed to regain their strength. Those who were sent off by themselves needed spare money for carfare out of the city. The men or women who acted as guides for the men to their next underground destination often had to be paid, too. And the people who housed the escapees turned to Edith Cavell when they needed extra food.

Suddenly the nurses noticed a startling change in their directress. Her light brown hair was gray! When had it happened? It was almost as if it had turned overnight. The slight figure was even thinner. Sadly they thought, she looks old—she is nearly fifty and she looks every year of it. They knew she was under great strain and admired her for her courage and spirit.

One thing that worried Edith, although she kept it to herself, was that the men she was hiding were growing careless. They were naturally tired of being confined; they longed to be out in the sunshine, to talk and be with others of their kind. When she let them out for exercise—duly bandaged and wrapped up— she could not always be sure they would not let out a stray word that would betray the Clinic. They discovered that next door to 149 was a small shop selling wine—Chez Jules, it was called. French soldiers liked to drop in there for a glass and comradely talk; English soldiers soon followed suit. It became a kind of rendezvous. The wine loosened tongues and stray bits of information percolated outside Chez Jules. It was no secret to the Germans after a while that the Clinic was harboring men other than hospital patients.

Across the street from 149 had been some empty lots. Now they were turned into potato fields where men often worked. Some of the men dropped in at the café now and then, mingling with the soldiers. After a time the nurses at 149 wondered about the men in the potato field. Were they spies? Miss Cavell told them not to imagine things. But the nurses could not overcome their fears. They were sure the men who worked there were watching who came and went at 149 and Chez Jules.

Capiau asked Edith if she could not do something to restrain the patients from talking and visiting the little restaurant. She said they were not animals to be caged. He tried to point out the risk she was running, but he could not convince her. Her sole concern was to keep them as safe as possible, to help them get well if they were ill, and to speed them on their way to freedom.

The guides who escorted the men to other houses or to the border were men who knew every street and bypath in Belgium. They took the men in groups of four or five, usually at night or in the late afternoon, and often the men were dressed as workingmen. They were given forged identification papers which the Princess de Croy had supplied. Since the German guards usually could not speak French, they were able to get away with little or no questioning. At first the guards along the border were old, semiretired soldiers. They did not like their tasks and were easily bribed. It might take days to reach the border, but once there it was not too difficult to cross into neutral Holland.

Once the Germans became suspicious that too many soldiers were escaping, however, they replaced the old guards with young troopers and strung up barbed wire and high-voltage fences. Snipers were hidden in trees, machine guns placed under hay-stacks. As it became harder to find a place to cross the border, the guides risked their lives with increasing frequency. Some took along a barrel with both ends knocked out so that the escaping soldier, hidden in the barrel, could be pushed under the barbed wire. Some had wire clippers and insulation blankets against the high voltage lines. But many a soldier died on his last night toward freedom. The Germans, as they proudly proclaimed, were determined "to continue this war until one can travel around the earth without seeing Englishmen who act as if they owned it."

The more hazardous escape became, the more determined Edith was to speed her soldiers to freedom. She was afraid to keep them long at the Clinic, and now people who had previously sheltered the men on their way to the border were afraid for their own lives.

The situation in Belgium had become perilous. Gas and electricity had been cut off; water had long since been rationed. Food grew scarcer daily. Edith was beside herself with worry about where money was coming from to keep her school going and to furnish the necessities for escaping soldiers.

Madame DePage called at the Clinic one day when Edith was going over her figures for a hundredth time. It was good to see her old friend, though there was only worry and sorrow to talk about. The reason for her visit, Madame explained, was that she was going to America to ask for funds. It was a dangerous journey across the submarine-infested ocean in the winter, but she was determined to do it. The hospitals were short of drugs and medicines and equipment. She was going to visit large cities and beg for help. It would take her several months, but she was sure that when she came back she would have the promise of assistance and money in hand to continue their work.

Edith herself brought up the question of what Dr. DePage might think of the way she was spending money at the nursing school. Madame DePage reassured her; the doctor had other things to think about and anyhow, she said, he would undoubtedly approve of what she was doing and how she was doing it. There was understanding between Edith and Madame DePage, as there had never been between

Edith and the doctor. She admired his skill and energy, but they never had got along well. The Ladies' Committee had practically washed its hands of the school, for the members did not approve of her assistance to Allied soldiers. So Edith was comforted by what Madame DePage said.

The copy of *La Libre Belgique* lying on her desk gave further comfort to Edith. She, as well as Madame DePage and many others, knew who was the moving spirit of the resistance paper. She had met him several times, and he had come to 149 Rue de la Culture. He was Philippe Baucq, a Brussels architect, and he was leading as dangerous a life as Edith. The Germans were still trying to learn his identity, but so far it had eluded them.

Many others were helping. Edith particularly admired the priest Père Meeus. She knew he was really a secret agent. A man of incredible courage, he had disguised himself as a pastry cook and taken a job in a German officers' club. There he had filched the plans of the raids by zeppelins and bombers on London and sent warnings to other agents by wireless hidden in various parts of Brussels.

The Germans were continually harassed by the Belgians. They would receive anonymous letters purporting to give information about some defector and rush to the spot, banging on the door and demanding that the suspect come out. When they broke down the door, the place might turn out to be an empty bathroom. Or they would be told that a key man in the underground was named André Vasalius and could be found at the Place des Barricades—only to find themselves confronting a public statue.

By such desperate means the Belgians tried to keep up their spirits and their defiance. But increasingly they paid with their lives for their courage.

CHAPTER

VIII

WITH THE COMING of spring, the reins were tightened on the restive Belgians. Strange, disturbing things began to happen at 149.

The Germans, determined to get at the root of Belgian resistance, sent one of their top secret police to Brussels to set up a criminal investigation office. One of these, Otto Mayer, a detective sergeant, called at the Clinic early in May. Sister Wilkins was sure she knew why he was there. She managed to keep him in conversation while she got word to three soldiers hiding in the rear room of the house that they must leave at once. Then she showed the sergeant all kinds of papers—food bills and plumber's statements and class records—anything she could lay her hands on that would take time and yet reveal nothing. Even so, he was not satisfied and took her to police headquarters.

She was calm under questioning; she knew nothing. They could not force her to incriminate herself or anyone at the school. At last, for lack of any evidence, they warned her sternly and let her go.

Verboten signs appeared all over the city now. It was a crime to harbor English or French soldiers on pain of death. But even this was not enough to stop those whose determination was as great as that of the Germans.

Tragedy came to 149 in May. Edith had taken a group of nurses to Antwerp to aid war casualties following the fall of the city. On her return she was told that the Germans had torpedoed the liner *Lusitania* off the coast of Ireland on its maiden trip, with a loss of 1,200 lives. One of those lost was Edith's friend Madame DePage.

The sinking of the *Lusitania*, more than any of the war stories that came to America from Europe, roused the people to a realization of what war meant. To Edith Cavell, it was one more evil act which had deprived her—and the world—of a gracious and lovely woman. The blow was bitter, personal.

She did not play the piano anymore. She seldom came to meals with the nurses. And she took to walking along the quiet streets of Brussels with her faithful Jack.

She had barely started out one June evening when two men approached her near the potato field. One was tall, good-looking, well-dressed, and he spoke French. He told her he was a French soldier seeking refuge for himself and his friend.

The Frenchman introduced himself as Georges

Gaston Quin, and his friend simply as Monsieur X. Edith did not question them; this sort of thing happened often. She turned home, taking the two men with her. Monsieur Quin she put with the other Frenchmen in the house, and Monsieur X with the English.

Next day Monsieur X left as unobtrusively as he had come. A guide named Gilles was taking him to Holland. Quin, however, said he was too ill to travel; he would stay to recuperate.

When Gilles returned from Holland he had disturbing news. Monsieur X had suddenly disappeared from the group. Gilles was sure he was a spy. Edith did not take the news seriously, however.

Georges Gaston Quin became a favorite of the house. His good looks and good humor brought new life to the sober surroundings and lifted the hearts of nurses and probationers. All seemed to fall under his spell. He was thoughtful, bringing little gifts to them when he ventured out, even bringing Sister Wilkins and Edith Cavell a bunch of flowers with a gracious speech of thanks for their kindness to him. Edith was touched by his act. But as soon as he had left the room, Sister Wilkins tossed the flowers on the floor and wiped her hands.

There was something queer about all this, she told the directress. She did not like him or his actions. Maybe he was a spy, too!

Edith refused to believe it. Then something occurred that shook her belief in him. Quin had taken a pretty nurse walking one evening. While they were gone, a German in uniform came to the house asking for a room for his son, who was ill.

Edith told him the Clinic was full—which was true, since she had five soldiers hidden in the back room. The German's manner indicated he did not believe her. While they talked he kept looking around, but he left without causing any trouble.

Edith could not disregard this. She knew why he had come and he would report whatever he had seen. The incident disturbed her more than anything else that had happened. She decided to ask the advice of Philippe Baucq, and penned a note which she sent to him by Jacqueline van Til, a probationer who had become a trusted friend.

On her way Jacqueline was startled to meet Quin. He was walking along a main avenue in broad daylight, as if he did not care whether he encountered German soldiers. He even asked Jacqueline to have a glass of wine with him. Panic-stricken, she refused and hurried on.

When she reached Baucq's house. Quin was sauntering along the opposite side of the street. He did not see her—or so she thought. Her heart was beating wildly. What should she do? She walked on slowly, and suddenly turned around to see if anyone was following her. There was someone—a man who had followed her after she met Quin. She stopped in front of a store window, waiting. The man passed her and walked on. But as she approached Baucq's house again she saw the man talking to a German officer.

That settled it. She was afraid now to go into

Baucq's house. She went to visit a friend instead, then wished she hadn't, for she learned her friend's husband and father had been arrested just a few hours previously for hiding French soldiers.

Jacqueline went back to the Clinic, badly frightened, and told Edith what had happened.

Edith sighed and said nothing. Above all she must keep calm, for her own sake as well as for her nurses, patients, and the soldiers she was helping.

One thing that lifted her spirits was the fact that a new clinic was being built. In spite of war and shortages of material and labor, it somehow was getting done. She liked to inspect it whenever she could.

Jacqueline went with her the following day on another inspection trip. She noticed that Edith spoke of others, not of herself—as if she would not be there or would have no role in the new Clinic.

"You must take care of this—" "You must see to that—". It struck Jacqueline as odd, but she dared not say anything in the face of Edith's calmness.

The weeks went by. When the building was nearly finished, Edith took them one by one to see the new offices and the rooms which she had chosen for them.

There were no further incidents until June 20, when a German officer came to 149 and asked to see the building. He went over it quickly, making no comments and departed with a click of his heels. Edith sighed with relief. Then she went through the rooms the officer had just inspected. In one of the bathrooms she stopped and drew in her breath sharply. On the floor lay the cap of an English soldier. The officer could not have failed to see it.

The next day two men came to the house. They wore civilian clothes and said they understood that the building would soon be vacated. They would like to see it with a view to renting it. Edith let them in. The men were polite and took their time going from room to room, measuring and talking in low tones as if they were making plans for converting it to their use.

Sister Wilkins burst into Edith's office when the men finally left. Her face was white. The men were Germans, she said excitedly. Edith asked how she knew. Sister Wilkins said she noticed they wore German army boots. And their eyeglasses were German-made!

It may have been true. Edith sometimes was too tired and harassed to notice or care. They waited a few days fearfully, but nothing happened. After a while they forgot the visit by the two men.

The spiriting away of soldiers went on, a never-ending work involving increasing danger. The Princess de Croy's group had more and more difficulty in doing its work. Guides were less anxious to risk their lives; too many had met death or been imprisoned when their daring plans failed. Philippe Baucq decided to lead a group into Holland himself. Though Edith and others tried to dissuade him, he said it was a job that must be done. They begged him to be careful, for he was too much needed; besides, he had a wife and children. But he was determined and managed to get two groups to safety in spite of the border patrols. It so happened that Georges Gaston Quin was in the first group. He was well now and, as he

said, ready to go. He thanked Edith and the others for their excellent care and promised to remember them always.

Escaped soldiers sometimes wrote Edith from safety in England and Holland. She was proud of their messages of gratitude, which proved her work had not been in vain. She did not realize they would be her undoing.

CHAPTER
IX

SISTER WILKINS and the nurses tried to talk Edith out of taking any more soldiers into the Clinic. It was far too dangerous; she had done more than her share. Let others take some of the risk now, they said.

But in July the Princess de Croy came to visit Edith. Most of the Allied soldiers had been conducted to the border, she reported, but now Louise Thuliez had found thirty more. They were in the woods near Cambrai. Edith knew why she was being told this. The Princess waited expectantly, hopefully.

Painfully Edith told her that the house was under suspicion. The whole underground movement was being watched. She pointed to a group of laborers in the potato field across the street. The same men, she said, had been there for days, doing practically nothing—merely watching to see who came and went at 149. The Princess nodded. The château was being watched too, she said. It was impossible to bring men there any more. Yet a place must be found for these men. Couldn't Edith take them in? Then, perhaps, there would be no need for further risks.

Finally Edith agreed. She never had turned away anyone. Nevertheless, she hoped she would be able to transfer these men almost at once to other houses in Brussels that were not so suspect. The Princess was deeply grateful. Brushing aside her gratitude, Edith told her how to leave the street, where to go, and how to act until she was safely out of the city. The Princess followed Edith's instructions, but when she returned to Mons she was arrested. In her bag was a letter from Edith Cavell. The police questioned her closely, and at last let her return to her château.

A short time later Quin appeared again at the Clinic. He said he had been approached by French authorities in Holland who asked him to serve as an intelligence agent for them. They had given him money for his work and assigned him to Brussels.

It sounded plausible. But no one believed him—Sister Wilkins least of all. She begged Edith to refuse him lodging and, to her own surprise, Edith agreed. Edith told him the house was full and he would have to find a place elsewhere. Although Sister Wilkins was relieved, she was not entirely satisfied and would not be until Edith gave up her work with the underground. It was far too nerve-racking for all of them, she said. Besides, food was scarce. Meat was almost impossible to find, and they lived on thin soups and bread and salad.

Nine soldiers came to the Rue de la Culture house on July 7. They were the first contingent of the group the Princess was sending. Edith put them in the first-floor back room because it had a door that led to the garden.

The nine soldiers had barely been installed when there was a knock at the door. Two German officers saluted and asked to speak to Miss Cavell. Sister Wilkins led them to her directress' office and then flew to the soldiers. Swiftly she led them through the basement and out to the back yard where she watched them climb over the garden wall to a vacant house. When she went back into the Clinic, other nurses were frantically gathering up English and French magazines and stuffing them under the bathtubs. As they stowed important papers in a storage tank beside the water closets, one of the officers tucked his head in the room and said sardonically, "*Verboten!*"

They stared at one another, open-mouthed. He was one of the two men who had talked about renting the Clinic building!

The officers had turned Edith's room upside down. Papers were strewn everywhere, the desk had been ransacked, closets emptied, floorboards had been pried up, pictures torn from the walls. Apparently the men did not find exactly what they were after, for eventually they went, leaving everyone in a state of near-collapse—all except Edith Cavell.

She remained calm, even remote. Sister Wilkins thought she was a kind of superhuman. But she begged Edith to destroy certain papers in case the officers came back, and Edith agreed. Sister Wilkins, feeling that at last she had made an impression, urged Edith to return to England. It was still possible, and she had done so much here she deserved to look after her own safety now.

Edith said calmly that she could not consider it. There were other English nurses at the Clinic for whom she was responsible, but she was not concerned about herself. Nor would she consider going into hiding in Belgium.

The search at 149 hurried matters up, however. The remaining English soldiers must be spirited way. José, the Armenian houseboy, himself took two of them to a store in the center of Brussels where the watchmaker owner would conduct them farther. One of the nurses took a few soldiers out of the city, too. She said afterwards she just strolled with them until they were out of danger.

But the Germans were not done with 149. They were determined to find the evidence which would give them reason for arrest. They stationed an inspector in a front room whose duty was to watch everyone who came or went at the house. Not to be outdone, the nurses set one of their own members to keep watch, too, from her room in the attic. She sat by the window in her nightgown, forcing herself to keep awake, for the safety of everyone depended on her.

70

It was nearly midnight when her watchfulness was rewarded. The three soldiers who had escaped over the wall earlier in the day were returning, somewhat the worse for wine, from Chez Jules! She rushed downstairs, casting a quick look into the room where the inspector sat. He was dozing! What luck! Quietly she opened the door and put her finger to her lips, pointing to the room and whispering, "*Le Boche*!" They stared at her a moment, then understood. She pointed to her bare feet, and silently they took off their shoes and followed her.

The nurse took them to Edith, who was praying beside her bed. Edith took the three soldiers through the garden and across town to Philippe Baucq's house. They were chastened soldiers now, realizing the danger they had brought on the house that had given them shelter. Edith left them in Baucq's care and walked back to the Clinic. It was six o'clock in the morning and the city was coming awake when she stepped inside and the German inspector stared at her. She joined the nurses at breakfast and led them in prayer. Then she climbed to her office again.

That day a man appeared asking for lodging and giving his name as Armand Jeannes. A week later, while Jeannes was still there, Quin came back and Edith let him stay the night.

The net was tightening. The nurses and probationers, not knowing what would happen next, started every time a bell rang or someone came to the door. They welcomed the distraction and hard work that moving from 149 to the new building entailed. It was difficult to find any kind of wagon or truck since everything had been commandeered by the Germans. So much of the moving was done by hand.

Nothing unusual happened during the remainder of July—nothing, at least, at 149. But in the office of the secret police an orderly plan was being put into effect. Lieutenant Bergan had Quin's report and decided that Philippe Baucq would be his first arrest. He reasoned that if Baucq were out of the way, the rest of the resistance might fall to pieces and no further arrests would have to be made.

For the work he chose Gustav Pincoffs, who selected three other men—Duisberg, Michel, and one who was referred to only as Plank II.

They were in no hurry. Day after day they watched Baucq's residence. On August 1, late in the evening, they were rewarded when Louise Thuliez came to spend the night with the Baucqs. Her usual lodging places were too dangerous now and she had been warned not to use them. She knew it was hazardous to come to the Baucqs, but she had to talk to him since there were still more men to be rescued. Baucq let her in, and while they talked of plans for spiriting away the men she helped him sort the most recent issue of *La Libre Belgique*.

Louise was still sorting and counting when Baucq took his dog for a walk. Soon after he left the house a detective stepped from the shadows and arrested him.

He knew he must try to warn Louise. Insisting that he had to go back to his house for something, he shouted loudly when he entered, "It's awful, whatever

it is!" He prayed that his voice would carry to the upstairs room where Louise and his family were working.

Louise heard him. Frantically she and Baucq's wife and daughters began throwing the papers out a rear window. But they reckoned without one of the policemen, who heard a strange sound, ran out of the house, and saw the flurry of descending papers.

Now they had evidence on Baucq and Thuliez. They found secret papers and other documents that Baucq had not destroyed, including many names and addresses of people connected with the resistance movement.

It was a rich haul. When they took Baucq and Louise to police headquarters, Lieutenant Bergan was gleeful. For he found, among Baucq's papers, a letter from Edith Cavell.

CHAPTER
X

WITH THE information they had in hand, the German secret police began rounding up resistance workers all over Belgium—miners, bakers, shopkeepers, people from all walks of life.

On August 3 the Prince de Croy made a quick trip to Brussels to see Edith Cavell. Despite the danger he was in himself, he wanted to warn her and others of their predicament.

Edith insisted that everything would be all right. She had destroyed all important papers, she said. Besides, they were moving—as he could see—and would soon be in their new home. In any event, she would not think of going into hiding.

The Prince looked at her in astonishment. Was it possible that she was really so calm and unconcerned? All Belgium, it seemed to him, was in a furor. Yet here sat this calm English nurse telling him he need not worry. He told her that Madame Bodart, who had hidden several dozen soldiers, already had been arrested. Edith took this news calmly too.

On August 4 three men called at the Clinic. They were English, they said, and wanted refuge. Edith explained that they were moving and suggested they get in touch with a man named Louis Severin, who might help them.

Louis Severin was arrested an hour later.

That same evening a German officer called and spent several hours interrogating Edith Cavell and Sister Wilkins. The nurses, busy about their moving, were nervous and upset. This, surely, was the end. Sister Wilkins, too, found it hard to keep her composure. She had told the officer that of course they had never received any communications from the London War Office. When that did not satisfy him, she had watched him go over the ledgers. The strain continued after he left. Who knew when the next blow would fall?

It came at half-past three the next afternoon when three men appeared at the Clinic and said they wanted to look at furniture. It sounded reasonable enough to Edith, who was eager to sell the pieces of furniture they were not moving. Any money they could realize would be a boon. When Sister Wilkins offered to show the men what was for sale, one of them held a revolver to her head and pushed her into a side room. He was Duisberg, who had arrested Baucq. As the other men started to look for Edith Cavell, several probationers came into the room. They were lined up, too, and told not to move.

Sister Wilkins tried to dart out of the room, but Duisberg grabbed her. She was only going to help Edith Cavell pack her clothes, she said. He let her go then.

The nurses and probationers waited. Sounds came softly to them—summer sounds through the open windows. Then came the sound of a car drawing up. At last the other two men pushed Edith Cavell into the room. She held her head high.

"Don't be so sad, my children," she said. "Everything will be all right. I will be back soon."

She was led into the waiting car. Sister Wilkins was put in another, which drew up behind it. Then they were driven away to police headquarters. The last thing Edith heard was her beloved dog Jack howling as if his heart would break.

The two women were questioned separately. Sister Wilkins steadfastly denied everything. Lieutenant Bergan, the trained questioner, could not break her story. She knew nothing—she knew nothing about anything. She had no idea that there had ever been young men hidden in the Clinic. She did not know about arrangements, about papers, about the people who called at the house. By eight o'clock that evening Lieutenant Bergan gave up. He released Sister Wilkins and she was returned to 149 Rue de la Culture.

The nurses swarmed around her, begging to know what had happened to Edith. But Sister Wilkins, exhausted and trembling from her ordeal, could not answer. She patted Jack and went to her room, wondering why she had been spared and when, if ever, she would see her dear Edith again.

In the morning a new edict was published in Brussels. Anyone hiding Englishmen or Frenchmen would receive the death penalty. One of the notices was tacked on the door of 149.

No one at the Clinic knew what had happened to Edith Cavell until five days later when a note came saying that Miss Cavell's clothes and bed linen could be brought to her at St. Gilles Prison. Food could be brought too.

Sister Wilkins and another nurse took clothes and provisions to the gray tomblike prison, but were not allowed to see Edith. All they learned was that she was prisoner number 23.

The move from the old to the new building went on, with Sister Wilkins now in charge. No one could take any joy in the event to which they had so long looked forward. The new building was cold and cheerless. It had no electricity, and the presence of German guards day and night cast gloom on everyone.

Nevertheless, the nurses wrote their directress about the move in glowing terms. They sent her favorite flowers, roses and chrysanthemums, but receiver no reply. They did not dare tell her that day and night Jack lay in front of the door of the room that was to have been hers, silent and brooding—not even whining.

Edith Cavell's first note from prison was written to Grace Jemmett:

My Dearest Grace:

I do hope you are not worrying about me. Tell everybody that I am quite all right here. I suppose from what I hear that I shall be questioned one of these days and when they have all they desire, I shall know what they mean to do about me. . . .

Is Sister Wilkins free? I have been thinking of her ever since last night.

Is Jackie sad? Tell him I will be back soon. The day is rather long. Can you send me a book, a little embroidery, my nail scissors and only a very few things as I have no place to put them. . . .

I will write again when there is anything to tell. Don't worry, we must hope for the best.

Part of the letter was torn and lost, but she had thought of everyone.

Not until September 14 did the worried nurses again get direct word from Edith. She wrote:

Your charming letter has given me such pleasure, and your beautiful flowers brought life and gay colors into my cell; the roses are still very fresh, but the chrysanthemums did not like prison life. They are like me; they cannot resist a very long time. . . .

The new term begins very soon; try to profit by your past experiences, always to be prompt, because the doctors do not like to wait for their pupils.

Everywhere in life we learn something new and if you were in my place you would soon realize how precious is liberty and how grateful we should be to have it.

We must all learn patience. It is not enough to be a good nurse only, but you should also be Christian women.

It seems that the new *clinique* is very nicely arranged. I hope I will see it soon and all my nurses as well.

Good-bye. Be wise and good.

A few days later when Sister Wilkins went to visit Edith Cavell, she found her pale and thin.

"At last the end has come," Edith told her. "I can't say I'm sorry; this waiting, waiting, this uncertainty has been a great strain. I have done what was my duty. They must do with me as they will."

She had changed. The iron will was still there, but hope seemed to have departed. In the beginning she had been sure she would be released. Now she realized that could not be. Resignation had taken the place of hope, but her calm was as great as ever.

Meanwhile, on August 31, the American Minister to Belgium, Brand Whitlock, wrote Baron von der Lancken, the German Political Minister in Brussels, saying he had just learned that Edith Cavell had been arrested. He asked the German Minister for permission to supply Edith with a lawyer for her defense. When Whitlock failed to receive a reply from the Baron, he wrote again on September 10. This time the Baron replied, saying that Edith Cavell had admitted concealing English, French and Belgian soldiers in her house and that her defense was in the hands of a lawyer named Braun. He refused to let the American Legation's lawyer, Monsieur Leval, visit Edith.

Life had become almost unbearably difficult in Brussels and throughout Belgium. Besides shortages of food and nearly everything else, the new German Military Governor—Lieutenant General von Sauberzweig—had made his motto "a horrible example" as the way to bring the Belgians under domination. He was merciless in his rule. He sent young and middle-aged people to work camps, forced others to stand in line to obtain identification papers, and in every way tried to humiliate as many people as possible.

Edith Cavell tried to keep busy in her cell. It had one window, high and barred, one gas jet, a metal cot, which became a table in the daytime, a straight-backed chair, a wooden wall cupboard, a crucifix, and a washbasin. The brick floor was cold and the hot-air vents were inadequate. She read her Bible and prayer book and made notes in her prayer book.

At some time she was alleged to have made a full confession. The people who questioned her told her that others connected with the resistance had confessed. Apparently she believed them. What must have happened is that each person said a few incriminating things, and when the Germans pieced these together they were able to get a full picture of the resistance and the people connected with it.

In her confession she gave a minute account of the number of soldiers she had harbored, the money that had been given her to spend for their care, how

81

she had used it, and from whom she had received it. She told explicitly how she had conducted soldiers to meeting places where guides took over; she told where the fleeing men had been transferred. She told of her various meetings with the Prince and Princess de Croy and Louise Thuliez and Philippe Baucq and Louis Severin and Madame Bodart.

It was a complete case against herself. Her defense lawyer, when he read it, groaned in anguish. How could he defend a woman who so precisely had implicated—and sentenced—herself?

CHAPTER
XI

OCTOBER 7, 1915 was a bright fall day. Two by two the accused were taken to the gate of grim St. Gilles prison. Motor buses transported them to the Parliament Building, where the trial was to be held.

The trial took place in the Senate chamber—an imposing room with murals of famous scenes in Belgian history on the walls, and rows of red-plush chairs catching the light from the tall windows. The prisoners were forced to sit with their backs to their counsels, a distinct disadvantage.

Edith Cavell was called first. Her appointed counsel, Mr. Braun, had been withdrawn and a new lawyer selected—a Mr. Sadi Kirschen, a Belgian. He had not met his client until the day of the trial and had prepared her defense merely from what he could hear and read. He seemed to think that there was nothing unusual in this. In fact, he said that if a trial proceeded slowly enough it was possible to get sufficient knowledge as it progressed to defend a prisoner.

Edith looked small and weary as she stood erect and calm before the judges. She had put aside her uniform, of which she was very proud, and on this day word a plain dress and coat and a dark hat on which were two feathers at an angle. Those who knew her wondered why she had chosen to appear in this costume instead of her uniform, which might have impressed the Germans with her dignity. But her friends decided she held her uniform and profession in such high esteem that she would not demean it. Yet without it, she seemed to have lost a certain superiority.

The prosecution read a further confession which Edith had signed and entered both confessions as evidence. When she was asked to reply, Edith said simply that she had only done her duty in trying to save men who might otherwise have died.

At noon pots of soup were brought in for the soldiers who guarded the prisoners during the noon recess. The prisoners were served nothing. Only a few had thought to save a bit of their prison fare for a noon meal; they shared the little they had with those who had none. Some of the guards offered them water from their own glasses, but all the prisoners refused to drink from the glasses. Instead, they poured a little water into their hands and drank it thirstily from their palms.

During the noon hour Edith managed to have a few words with Louise Thuliez. She, Louise, Baucq, and Capiau had not much chance, she thought. Though she believed they would not be shot, they would probably be sent to work camps at hard labor. They had done what they had done from a patriotic sense of duty; surely nothing but prison or hard work would be the punishment for that.

The trial dragged on till seven that night. The next morning it resumed, with the prisoners weary, bedraggled, and apprehensive. One by one they were called up and the charges read against them. The questions were put in German and translated into French.

When it was Edith's turn, her lawyer, Kirschen, made his defense. He pleaded that she had given her life to the service of humanity. He described her work early in the war and how she had cared for German soldiers as tenderly as she had for those of other nationalities. She was dedicated to her profession, and now she was a victim of circumstance.

It made no impression on the judges. The Military Prosecutor, a dapper man with high color and a waxed moustache, said that no doubt she might have felt that way about English soldiers, but she must acknowledge that Belgian soldiers would have been free to stay without danger.

One of the judges told her she was foolish to have helped Englishmen. They were an ungrateful lot.

Edith denied this.

How did she know they were not ungrateful?

They had sent her letters and notes from England, she said. They thanked her for helping them. Her lawyer knew that her case was hopeless when she made that statement. She had signed her own death warrant. She told the court, without a quaver, that she had sent about two hundred men on their way to freedom.

When Edith was asked, "What have you to say in your defense?" she replied stonily:

"Nothing!"

The prisoners were taken back to St. Gilles again, and on October 11, a rainy, gloomy day, they were returned to the Parliament Building to hear their sentences.

The Military Prosecutor opened a briefcase bulging with papers. In the silence of the chamber he read:

"The tribunal is of the opinion, partly on the strength of their own statements, and partly on the strength of the assertions of their fellow prisoners, that the following are the chief organizers: Prince de Croy (escaped), Philippe Baucq, Louise Thuliez, Edith Cavell, Countess Jeanne de Belleville, Louis Severin."

He paused a moment and then said in a voice that echoed in the solemn chamber:

"For all of them, death!"

Baucq turned deathly pale. But Edith Cavell stood against a wall, upright, calm, impassive. Capiau and Ada Bodart were among those sentenced to fifteen years at hard labor. The Princess de Croy drew ten years at hard labor. She, at least, knew that her husband was safe in Holland.

One of the men went to Edith and urged her to appeal the sentence. He felt sure that if she begged for mercy she would be given it.

But Edith shook her head. "It is useless. I am English. And they want my life."

The commandant of the prison came and escorted Edith back to her cell.

That evening the nurses, waiting nervously in the new Clinic for some kind of news, had their last hopes destroyed. The lawyer for Dr. DePage's Institute had heard of the grim sentence and came to tell them.

"When?" they asked.

"Tomorrow at five o'clock in the morning," he replied. "Or maybe as early as two."

They could not believe it. There must be something they could do! They must stretch every nerve, follow every slightest chance. Sister Wilkins threw on her cloak and another nurse, Miss Smith, accompanied her to the prison. The warden would not let them in. He was sympathetic, but there was nothing he could do. Why didn't they go to see Monsieur Leval, he suggested?

They hurried to Leval's house. He was writing another note to the American Minister about Edith Cavell. He, too, was utterly astonished and unbelieving. This couldn't be! This must not happen!

He, Sister Wilkins and Miss Smith set out for the Legation. There Whitlock, sick in bed, sent for Hugh

Gibson, the young Secretary, who was dining out. Leval and Whitlock drafted a letter to Baron von der Lancken, setting forth in the strongest terms why he should grant a pardon to Edith Cavell.

While they waited for Gibson, the Reverend Gahan, who was at the American Ministry, set out for St. Gilles. When Gibson came, he and Leval contacted the Dutch Ambassador, Maurice van Vollenhoven— who decided he could not do anything because of Holland's neutrality—and the Spanish Ambassador, the Marquis de Villobar. Though the Marquis had wooden legs, a withered hand, and a bald head, he was a brave fighter.

The three rushed to the German Political Ministry, which was dark. They pounded on the door. When the concierge finally answered, he said the Baron was at the theatre. They gave him their car and urged him to fetch von der Lancken at once. There wasn't a moment to lose . . .

Meanwhile, Father Gahan made his way to Edith's cell. She rose and greeted him calmly. They talked for almost an hour while she sat on her neatly made-up cot and he on a chair beside her.

"I have no fear or shrinking," she told him. "I have seen death so often it is not strange or fearful to me. I expected it would end thus. I thank God for this ten weeks' quiet before the end . . . life has always been hurried and full of difficulty. This time of rest has been a great mercy."

It struck the Reverend Gahan forcibly how small she was, how pale and thin. While in prison she had lost a great deal of weight, but her eyes were clear and unafraid.

"They have all been very kind to me here," she said. "But this I would say standing as I do in view of God and eternity. I realize that patriotism is not enough. I must have no hatred or bitterness toward anyone."

They talked for a time, then knelt together on the cold floor and recited the Lord's Prayer and one of Edith's favorite hymns, "Abide with me; fast falls the eventide. . . ."

The Reverend Gahan did not think he could bear to leave her alone, but their time together was up.

"Perhaps I had better go now. You must rest," he said.

"Yes," Edith replied. "I have to be up at five A.M."

He said good-bye, and she told him:

"We shall meet again."

When he had gone, Edith finished making notes in her Bible and her prayer book, which had been her comfort during the long days of imprisonment. The German commandant had her letter, the last one she would write to her nurses. She hoped it would reach them.

MY DEAR NURSES:

It is a very sad moment for me when I write to make my adieus to you. It calls to mind the fact that the 17th September was the end of eight years of my direction of the school. I was so happy to be called to aid in the organization of the work that our committee had just founded. The 1st October of the year 1907 there were only four young students; now we are already numerous—between 50 and 60 in all, I believe, counting those who have received their diplomas and have already left the school. . . .

In your beautiful house you will have more patients and you will have all that is necessary for their comfort and your own.

To my regret I have not been able always to speak very much with you personally; you know that I have had a good many occupations, but I hope you will not forget our evening chats. I told you that devotion would give you real happiness— and the thought that before God and yourselves you have done your entire duty with a good heart will be your greatest comfort in the hard moments of life and in the face of death. . . .

If there is one among you whom I have wronged, I beg you to forgive me; I have been perhaps too severe sometimes but never voluntarily unjust, and I have loved you all much more than you thought.

My best wishes for the happiness of all my girls, those who have left the school as well as those who are there still, and thank you for the kindness you have always shown me.

Your devoted Directress,
EDITH CAVELL

Back at political headquarters the desperate little party waited out the hours. At ten-thirty von der

Lancken returned from his gay evening. He was surprised to find them there. Gibson tried to persuade him that minutes were precious, but von der Lancken said that if the news was not official it could not be true. He refused to believe it. It was too late to do anything now, he insisted. But the members of the party, weary and furious, were just as insistent. He must telephone the presiding judge of the court-martial. When he came back into the room he was not quite so cocky. Yes, it was true . . . Miss Cavell would be shot that night. The hour? Perhaps two . . . perhaps later.

Gibson presented Brand Whitlock's letter. Von der Lancken read it without emotion. Edith Cavell was a spy, he said; she must be shot. Angrily Gibson refuted that. She was not a spy—she had not even been charged with spying. She was serving humanity. She had saved the lives of German soldiers as well as Allied.

One of von der Lancken's aides said brutally, "The life of one German soldier is more important than that of all the old English nurses."

Von der Lancken told the men they should go home and get some sleep. In the morning they could talk about it.

But in the morning it would be too late, they said. He himself had admitted it.

They brought all the arguments to bear that they could. They spoke with passion and fire. They reminded von der Lancken of the burning of Louvain and the sinking of the *Lusitania*. This action would turn the world against the Germans even more. They could not execute a woman—a nurse!

Von der Lancken insisted that nothing could be done. It was late. They might as well go home. They demanded that he call the Kaiser. Von der Lancken paled at the very thought. Then call on the Military Governor! Ask for a delay!

With every minute precious, they finally wore him down. He agreed to go to von Sauberzweig's house, and they sat down again to wait. Eleven-thirty . . . eleven-forty-five . . . twelve o'clock.

Von der Lancken returned at last and told them:

"The Military Governor has decided that the death penalty must be inflicted. He will not change his decision."

The Marquis de Villobar seized the German by the coat. "It is insane—this thing you are doing! Her blood will be on your head!"

He got hold of himself then and the three men tried to get von der Lancken to use his influence to win a stay of execution. They urged him again to appeal to the Governor, to the Kaiser. It was no use.

In the dark and the rain they went out to the Legation car, and the heavy door of the Political Ministry closed behind them.

It was already tomorrow.

CHAPTER
XII

IT WAS four-thirty in the morning. The rain had stopped but the streets were still wet and a gray mist hung over the city.

When the German army chaplain came with the guard to knock on Edith Cavell's cell door, she was ready. She had fixed her cot and put away her things. Her hair was neatly combed, and she wore a plain black dress, her blue nurse's cloak, and a black hat.

A matron came and asked if she would have a cup of tea. Edith refused it. With a firm step she walked down the cold corridor, the chaplain beside her, a guard in front and a guard behind her.

Outside the prison a gray military sedan was waiting. Beside the gate the agonized faces of Sister Wilkins and Jacqueline van Til pressed against the railing, searching for one last glimpse of their beloved directress. She did not turn her head, and they knew she had not seen them. Pressing their hands to their mouths to silence their sobbing, they went to the Clinic.

The sedan drove swiftly in the pale dawn to the Tir National, the Belgian rifle range. Edith walked down the corridor of the old building, and then stopped a moment. She opened her prayer book. In it she had already written:

Court-martialed 7th Oct. 1915
Condemned to death 8th Oct. in the Salle des
    Députés at 10:30 A.M. with 7 others.

Now she added one last item:

Died at 7 A.M. on Oct. 12th, 1915
With Love to My Mother

E. Cavell.

Then, before she moved on, she asked for several safety pins. Although no one knew why she wanted them, the request was granted and after a brief delay the pins were handed to her. She stooped down and pinned her skirts around her ankles. She was afraid that when she was shot her skirts would fly up.

She walked with composure to the shooting range. They led her to a post and tied and blindfolded her. Fifteen feet away Philippe Baucq was tied to another post.

The chaplain took his farewell. The command "Fire!" rang out. The shots from the firing squad passed through her body and she slumped to the ground, the sound of the volley echoing from the stone wall.

The commander stepped to her, saw that she still was alive, and fired one final bullet into her temple.

Edith Cavell was dead.

They buried her without ceremony in the grounds of the Tir National. There her body lay for nearly four years.

After the end of the war her body was brought to England on board the battleship *Rowena*. The flag-draped casket was carried through streets lined with respectful crowds. The Queen waited in Westminster Abbey where services were held. Then, at her family's request, the body of Edith Cavell was taken home to Norwich.

Not many people in the world had heard of Edith Cavell before October 12, 1915. But after that everyone knew of her. Men enlisted by the thousands to avenge her death. America entered the war to fight beside England. The gentle nurse became a symbol of right against might, her life an inspiration, her death a challenge.

The work she started lives on as a timeless memorial to her. A fine Edith Cavell–Marie DePage Institute rose in Brussels. The nursing service she started has grown and flourished. The hospitals where she trained and served in England have grown and improved and increased their services to mankind. Sister Wilkins carried on her work at the Institute with Edith Cavell's memory fresh before her.

In faraway Canada a beautiful mountain was named for Edith Cavell. In Colorado an imposing glacier bears her name. In Paris, in the Tuileries, there is a bas-relief of the famous nurse. And in Trafalgar Square, in the heart of busy London, men still take off their hats as they pass the dignified shaft erected to her.

Jack dozed away his life at the Château de Bellignies, perhaps dreaming of his beloved mistress who was at rest at last. Truth and duty had been her staff. When she laid it down, her students carried it forward into the world.

The Author

This biography of Edith Cavell is the fifty-sixth book which Adele DeLeeuw has published—and one she long has looked forward to writing. Miss De-Leeuw, a native of Hamilton, Ohio, lives in Plainfield, New Jersey. Besides her books, some written in collaboration with her sister Cateau DeLeeuw, she has published many articles, short stories and poems.

INDEX